Gallery Books
Editor: Peter Fallon

THE ENEMY WITHIN

Brian Friel

THE ENEMY WITHIN

Gallery Books

The Gallery Press published
The Enemy Within in paperback
and hardback in 1979.
This edition published 1992.

The Gallery Press
Loughcrew
Oldcastle
County Meath
Ireland

ISBN 0 902996 92 4

    The Gallery Press receives financial assistance from An Chomhairle Ealaíon / The Arts Council, Ireland.

Preface

The Enemy Within is neither a history nor a biography but an imaginative account, told in dramatic form, of a short period in St. Columba's thirty-four years of voluntary exile. I have avoided the two spectacular and better known aspects of the saint — the builder of monasteries in Ireland and in Scotland, and the prophet and miracle worker, both of which are described generously in St. Adamnan's *Life* — and have concentrated instead on the private man.

When I have relied on specific events of the time, I have tried to be accurate. The scholar may object to many liberties I have taken but particularly to my translation of old names into their modern equivalents (e.g. Hy is here Iona, Dalraida is County Antrim, Cinel Eoghain is split into County Derry and County Tyrone, the Scotland and England in the text are the countries as we know them), but I felt that once I put modern prose into the mouths of the characters, geographical alterations were necessary too.

When Columba first went to Iona he brought with him twelve followers among whom were Grillaan, Caornan, Dochonna and Diarmuid. Little or nothing is recorded of these four so that my treatment of them is purely speculative.

When considering these days, one should remember that they were violent and bloody, that Columba was reared 'among a people whose Constitution and National Construction rendered civil faction almost inseparable from their existence' (Reeves), and that it was not until 804, over two hundred years after Columba's death, that monastic communities were formally exempted from military service.

Brian Friel

Characters

COLUMBA, Abbot of Iona
GRILLAAN, Prior
DOCHONNA, domestic manager
CAORNAN, copyist
DIARMUID, personal attendant to Abbot
   All these five were founder members and priests
BRENDAN, farm manager (priest)
OSWALD, novice
BRIAN, messenger
EOGHAN, Columba's brother
AEDH, Eoghan's son

Time and place

The year 587 — autumn. The island of Iona, off the west coast of Scotland.

ACT ONE: Autumn afternoon
ACT TWO: Three weeks later
ACT THREE: Two weeks later

Set

The action throughout takes place in Columba's cell. It is an austere, comfortless apartment furnished with a few stools, a stone bed covered with straw, a stone pillow (right), a large wooden table (left). On the wall above the table hangs a collection of scrolls — the equivalent of a library.
   The monks wear a heavy woollen robe of natural colour. It has a hood. They wear sandals. Columba's robe is of the same rough texture but is white.

The Enemy Within was first produced by the Abbey Theatre, Dublin, at the Queen's Theatre on 6 August 1962, with the following cast:

COLUMBA	Ray McAnally
GRILLAAN	Philip O'Flynn
DOCHONNA	Micheál Ó hAonghusa
CAORNAN	Micheál Ó Briain
DIARMUID	Geoff Golden
OSWALD	Vincent Dowling
BRIAN	Patrick Laffan
BRENDAN	Eóin Ó Suilleabháin
AEDH	T. P. McKenna
EOGHAN	Edward Golden

Play produced by Ria Mooney
Setting by Tomás MacAnna
Stage management by Bert Carroll

The orchestra under the direction of Seán Ó Riada performed the following selections:

Overture	*Idomeneo*	Mozart
First interval	*Lyric Suite*	Grieg
Second interval	*Ceol Gaedhealach*	Ó Riada

for Bobby Toland
in friendship

ACT ONE

An autumn afternoon in Columba's room. The monk CAORNAN, *who is a scribe, is working at the large wooden table. He is a frail old man of seventy-one years. His eyesight is weak. He stops occasionally to rub his eyes. He is pale and gentle and soft-spoken.* DOCHONNA *enters. He is sixty-six. His manner is brusque but there is a deep attachment between* CAORNAN *and himself. They look on themselves as the old fellows of the community. The monk* DOCHONNA *is domestic manager — in charge of the kitchen. He is deaf.*

DOCHONNA Where is he?

CAORNAN Out giving a hand with the corn. He said he wouldn't be long.

    DOCHONNA *grunts and glances at Caornan's work.*

DOCHONNA When did you start working in his room?

CAORNAN The day before yesterday. My own room faces north. Too dark.

DOCHONNA More light here?

CAORNAN (*Nodding in agreement*) That's it. Yes.

DOCHONNA How are the eyes?

CAORNAN Grand, thanks, Dochonna. And your hearing?

DOCHONNA What's that?

CAORNAN (*Pointing to his own ears*) The hearing — how is it?

DOCHONNA Nothing wrong with my hearing. Whatever about the rest of you, thank God I have all my faculties about me.

CAORNAN We're getting no younger.

DOCHONNA I'll tell you something, Caornan: I'm younger than he is. Did you know that?

CAORNAN I thought you and he were both sixty-six?

DOCHONNA There's something you never knew before, eh?

CAORNAN (*Contents himself with nodding*) Yes, yes. (*It is a strain to*

DOCHONNA *keep shouting to* DOCHONNA)
And if he thinks he's young enough at sixty-six to be out at the corn, then he should allow his juniors to be out at it too. There now.

He goes to the door as if he is about to leave, stops and comes back again.

Of course I can understand him keeping you at your work, Caornan. You're a much older man.

CAORNAN You know very well I'm seventy-one.

DOCHONNA But me that's younger than him — you never knew that before, did you now?

CAORNAN *shakes his head: No, no.*

He was born on the 7th of December, 521, and I was born on the 11th of December, 521. You see?

CAORNAN You're only a young fellow, Dochonna.

DOCHONNA Four days younger — much as he would like to forget it. Huh! Out there slogging like one of the novices!

CAORNAN He likes to be out and to be active.

DOCHONNA What's that?

CAORNAN He's very strong, very energetic.

DOCHONNA Four full days between us. I'm younger than either of you.

CAORNAN What are you preparing for next Sunday?

DOCHONNA Eh?

CAORNAN Next Sunday — the feast day of Finnian of Clonard.

DOCHONNA I know that.

CAORNAN What are you giving us? (*Points to his mouth*) Food.

DOCHONNA That's what I want to see him about — to get permission to go out to Tiree for a sheep.

CAORNAN Lovely.

DOCHONNA A sheep.

CAORNAN (*Nodding*) Yes. Very nice.

The young monk BRENDAN *bursts in. He is the farmer. He holds the skirts of his habit up around his knees because he has been running. He is a very powerful young man.*

BRENDAN   Columba — where is he?

CAORNAN   Out at the harvest, Brendan.

BRENDAN   The cow — the cow — she's calved in the lower meadow — a wee beauty — strong as a horse —

BRENDAN *dashes off again.*

DOCHONNA   Him and those bees of his! They're either swarming or stinging him!

CAORNAN   It's the cow, Dochonna. She's calved at last.

DOCHONNA   (*Recovering*) The cow has calved. I know that, Caornan. I'm not deaf. I just mentioned the bees in passing.

CAORNAN   Yes, Dochonna.

DOCHONNA   I'd better get back to my work. There are so many foreigners about the place these times that if you turn your back for five minutes, they're slipping garlic or some other poison into the food.

As he is about to leave, GRILLAAN *and* OSWALD *enter.* GRILLAAN *is Prior, second in command to* COLUMBA. *He is in his sixties but straight and well preserved. He is a calm, balanced man and his opinions are respected by the other monks.* OSWALD *is new to Iona — a novice. He speaks with a pronounced English accent. He is very ardent, very tense, very eager to throw himself into his new life.* GRILLAAN *is showing him around.*

GRILLAAN   And this is Columba's room — our Abbot.

CAORNAN *rises to greet the newcomer.*

A new novice, Oswald, all the way from the south coast of England. (*Introducing him*) Dochonna, who is our house manager and sees that we get enough to eat —

DOCHONNA   You're welcome, boy.

OSWALD   Thank you very much.

13

GRILLAAN And Caornan, our scribe, and one of the best Greek scholars in Europe.

CAORNAN Don't listen to the Prior, son. I hope you're happy with us.

OSWALD Are all the monks old men?

GRILLAAN (*Laughs*) Heavens, no, boy! I've introduced you only to what's left of the founder members of Iona — Caornan and Dochonna here; and Columba and Diarmuid we met outside, and myself — yes, five survivors from the original twelve. But there are scores of young men from all over the world: French and German and Italian and Spanish and, of course, Irish — from all over the place. Don't worry; you'll have plenty of company.

OSWALD This is a comfortable room.

GRILLAAN (*Indulgently*) Yes — Columba insists on fresh straw on his stone bed.

CAORNAN How long have you been travelling, Oswald?

OSWALD About eight days. Father came with me the length of the mainland.

CAORNAN I'm sure he's lonely now whoever sees him. And your mother too.

OSWALD As a matter of fact, he was very sensible about it all. (*To* GRILLAAN) When do I begin?

GRILLAAN Time enough, son. You'll spend a day or two just looking around, getting to know the island and our routine here. You have all your life before you.

CAORNAN Is there any particular work you like, Oswald?

OSWALD I hope to be a scribe.

CAORNAN I'm sure you'll be a good scribe.

DOCHONNA (*To* OSWALD) Did you ever hear tell of a place called Lough Conn, in Connaught?

OSWALD I am English — from the south of England.

DOCHONNA No, no, not England, Connaught, in the west of Ireland. That's where I come from — Lough Conn.

OSWALD *looks to* GRILLAAN.

GRILLAAN (*To* OSWALD) He is deaf. (*To* DOCHONNA) This boy is from the south of England, Dochonna.

DOCHONNA Aw — another foreigner.

GRILLAAN (*To* OSWALD) He sounds gruff but he's really very kind.

> COLUMBA *enters, followed by* DIARMUID. COLUMBA *is sixty-six but looks a man sixteen years younger. There is vitality, verve, almost youthfulness in every gesture. He has an open healthy face. He looks for no subservience from his community; they are like brothers together. When he comes on, the atmosphere is breezy and vital. He is followed by* DIARMUID, *fat and puffy, his personal attendant.* DIARMUID *is a crank; he is constantly worried about his health. As they come on,* DIARMUID *is panting behind his Abbot and trying helplessly to pick the straws off Columba's habit.*

COLUMBA (*To* OSWALD) I'm sorry for keeping you but we had to get the field stooked before the light fails. Have you met everybody?

> *From the moment* COLUMBA *comes on,* OSWALD's *eyes never leave him.*

OSWALD Only the old men, Columba.

COLUMBA (*Laughing heartily*) And that describes them all right! Aren't they a depressing sight? Grillaan here isn't so bad — although he's no fledgling either. But as for Caornan and Dochonna, it's near time they got their reward, the poor souls. And you can see yourself Diarmuid here is killed trying to keep up with me.

DOCHONNA Columba —

COLUMBA What is it, Dochonna?

DOCHONNA Have I your permission to go to Tiree for a sheep?

COLUMBA Have we a feast this week?

CAORNAN Next Sunday is the thirty-eighth anniversary of Finnian's death.

COLUMBA Thirty-eight years — is it that length?

GRILLAAN It seems like a year at most.

COLUMBA The times we had there in Meath, do you remember?

	Brendan and Colman and Canice —
GRILLAAN	And Ciaran —
COLUMBA	And Ciaran. And do you remember young Comgall with the black eyes and the innocent face?

They have all been in Finnian's monastery together. This is an old joke of theirs.

GRILLAAN	'Why are you working in the forge, Comgall?'
COLUMBA	'Because I was picked, Finnian.'
GRILLAAN	'You are a Christian now, not a Pict. Get out!'

They all laugh at this — all except OSWALD. DOCHONNA *laughs too although he is not sure what he is laughing at.*

COLUMBA	And the day Enda came from Aran, do you remember?
CAORNAN	With the cart-load of dulse! I remember that!
DIARMUID	Don't mention it. I was sick for a week after.
GRILLAAN	'So thoughtful of you, Enda. A load of manure — the very thing we need.'
COLUMBA	I thought Enda would die laughing.
DIARMUID	They claimed they could hear him in Kildare, remember?
GRILLAAN	But old Finnian, the shrewd fox, he didn't bat an eye. 'Dulse? Oh, yes, I have heard of it. My mother used to give it to the young pigs.'
DIARMUID	Never stuck for an answer. Never.
DOCHONNA	Do you remember the day he found young Comgall in the forge?
COLUMBA	We were just talking about that, Dochonna.
DOCHONNA	What's this it was he said? 'Out you go, boy. I didn't choose you for iron work and you're a Christian now.' (*Chuckles*)
DIARMUID	No. No, no, Dochonna. You've messed it all up.
DOCHONNA	What's that? What's he saying?
COLUMBA	It was a good one, wasn't it, Dochonna? And what was it he used to call you? 'The Hardy Trout' — wasn't that it?

DOCHONNA (*Delighted*) Aye, aye, aye. On account of Lough Conn. Aye, 'The Hardy Trout'. So well you remember, Columba, eh?

COLUMBA I remember everything. The beech trees and the chestnuts and the oaks and the flat, green plains and the silver of the Boyne water on a good summer's day. And the day he died, I remember too. I was in Derry at the time — you were there too, Grillaan — and I remember I was in the chapel saying a mouthful of prayers and — (*He breaks off because the memory embarrasses him*) — He was a good man, Finnian; a good man.

OSWALD What happened in the chapel?

GRILLAAN He knew that Finnian had died. He told me when he came out. We didn't get word until two days later.

OSWALD (*Intensely to* COLUMBA) You had a vision? An angel appeared to you? What happened? How did you know he was dead?

COLUMBA Here! How did we get away back into the past like that? Do you know, Oswald, these old doters will soon have me as bad as themselves. Did you have anything to eat yet?

OSWALD I had a meal at noon. I don't want anything more today.

COLUMBA You'll eat when you're told to; and I'm telling you now. Take him off with you, Dochonna, and give him as much as he can hold. (DOCHONNA *does not understand*) Food. Plenty.

OSWALD With your permission, Columba, I would prefer not to eat. The Prior tells me you allow yourself only one small meal each day. I wish to do exactly as you do.

COLUMBA I eat once a day for two very good reasons, son: Dochonna's cooking and my own stomach. You might as well know that both Diarmuid and myself are very bad stomach cases.

The others laugh at this.

DIARMUID That's not fair, Columba. Apart from the run at Mull last Friday, I haven't been seasick for a week.

COLUMBA   Argyll the day before yesterday?

DIARMUID   There was a gale blowing then. Everyone was sick except yourself.

DOCHONNA   Come on, lad. Come on.

COLUMBA   (*To* OSWALD) And after you've eaten, come and see me. We'll have a chat then.

DOCHONNA   Is it all right if I go to Tiree, Abbot?

COLUMBA   By all means, Dochonna, and choose the fattest you can get. Yes, yes. Go, go.

> As DOCHONNA *and* OSWALD *go towards the door,* BRENDAN *charges in as before.*

BRENDAN   Columba! — Columba! — Another calf! — A second! — Twins! Two of them.

COLUMBA   Another?

BRENDAN   She's had one already — a regular bull —

COLUMBA   Good for you, Brendan! You always said she was a good cow, that!

BRENDAN   Give me a hand with them, Diarmuid. The men are all at the corn.

DIARMUID   Me?

COLUMBA   Go on, man. Let them see the fine substantial community they have joined.

> BRENDAN *and* DIARMUID *go off.* GRILLAAN *goes towards the door.*

GRILLAAN   I've never seen twin calves in all my life.

COLUMBA   And listen, Grillaan —

GRILLAAN   Yes?

COLUMBA   Tell Brendan he's to go to bed for the rest of the day. He's been up with the cow for the past two nights.

GRILLAAN   He doesn't like the bed any more than yourself.

COLUMBA   Whether he likes it or not. And Grillaan —

> GRILLAAN *halts at the door.*

Don't put that new novice into the end cell.

GRILLAAN   Why not? The last in always uses it. That's the tradition.

COLUMBA He comes of wealthy people and was used to every luxury. We must wean him slowly.

GRILLAAN You're the Abbot.

GRILLAAN goes off.

CAORNAN He will make a good monk, Columba.

COLUMBA stretches himself. Between CAORNAN and himself there is a special intimacy.

COLUMBA Oswald? Too early to say yet.

CAORNAN No, he has clean eyes and the smell of courage about him.

COLUMBA If he's strong enough for the life here, Caornan.

CAORNAN He hopes to be a scribe.

COLUMBA We have a scribe — the best there is. How is it going?

COLUMBA goes to the table to look at the work.

CAORNAN I'm at Chapter 10, Verse 37.

COLUMBA You find it easier to work here?

CAORNAN My eyes don't tire as easily. As long as I'm not in your way.

COLUMBA I'm glad to have you, man. You're company for me. Let's see today's work.

CAORNAN I got only four verses done today.

COLUMBA picks up the scroll and looks at it.

COLUMBA Beautiful, beautiful, beautiful.

CAORNAN (*Childishly pleased*) You like it?

COLUMBA Exquisite, Caornan Mac Ua Soghain. Exquisite.

CAORNAN I'm inclined to go off the lines now —

COLUMBA (*Reading*) 'Do not think that I come to send peace upon earth; I come not to send peace but the sword. For I come to set a man at variance against his father and the daughter against her mother and the daughter-in-law against her mother-in-law. And a man's enemies shall be they of his own household. He that loveth father or mother more than Me is not worthy of Me — '. A man's enemies — they of his own household —

CAORNAN That epsilon — I blotted it slightly.

COLUMBA Caornan, you must pray for me, Caornan.

CAORNAN *looks at him.*

Because I need your prayers; because I am ringed with enemies.

CAORNAN Enemies? You?

COLUMBA Because I am not worthy of Him.

CAORNAN Abbot!

COLUMBA Out at the corn there, Cormac was cutting, and I was behind him tying, and the sun was warm on my back, and I was stooped over, so that this bare, black exile was shrunk to a circle around my feet. And I was back in Tirconaill; and Cormac was Eoghan, my brother, humming to himself; and the dog that was barking was Ailbe, our sheep-dog; and there were trees at the bottom of the field as long as I did not look; and the blue sky was quick with larks as long as I did not lift my head; and the white point of Errigal mountain was behind my shoulder as long as I kept my eyes on the ground. And when we got to the bottom of the field, Cormac called to me, 'Look what I found! A horse-shoe! That's for luck!' But I did not look up because he was still Eoghan, my brother, and the earth was still Gartan earth; and the sound of the sea was the water of Gartan Lough; and any minute Mother would come to the head of the hill and strike the iron triangle to summon us in for food. And when Cormac spoke I did not answer him because I could not leave them, Caornan. As God is above, I could not leave them!

CAORNAN There is a layman in every priest, Columba.

COLUMBA But I am old, Caornan. And virtue has not grown with the years. And when He sends for me, He will find me as naked as I was when Etchen imposed hands on me in Clonfad.

CAORNAN Your monasteries — all over Ireland — at least a score of them. And here in Scotland, as many more. You are famous, Columba, all over the Christian world. Your name is spoken with reverence in Rome itself.

COLUMBA As a builder of churches! As a builder of schools! As an organiser! But the inner man — the soul — chained irrevocably to the earth, to the green wooded earth of Ireland! (*He becomes conscious of his intensity and pretends to laugh*) I'll tell you a funny thing I heard the last time I was over there — when was it? Easter a year? Anyhow, I was visiting the Derry house and I was speaking to a young monk, a neighbour of our own, a young lad from Kilmacrenan, who was about to be sent to France on mission work. And in the course of conversation I said to him, 'You'll miss Derry and the Foyle and the hills?' and he blushed, this young lad, and he said to me, 'I won't, Patronus.' 'What?' I said. 'Not even a little?' And he became more and more confused and eventually he stammered, 'I've — I've taken the cure!' 'Cure?' 'Yes,' he said. 'Before I left home, I spent a night on the Flag of Columba.'

CAORNAN What's that?

COLUMBA That's what I said. It appears that one night, years and years ago, on my way home from Slieve League, I slept on this great slab of rock. Needless to say, I don't remember doing it. But it seems that ever since a pious practice has grown round the spot and all the young Tirconaill emigrants spend their last night there. And this is the funny part — by doing this they are guaranteed to be freed from home-sickness and longing for their native land! Ironical, isn't it?

CAORNAN It could well be. I wouldn't mock at it.

COLUMBA I'll tell you the explanation: the night on the rock paralyses them with rheumatism and when they do remember Tirconaill afterwards, they curse it to the depths of hell! (COLUMBA *laughs heartily at his joke*)

CAORNAN Columba, there is something I wish to ask you. I have been trying to gather courage for the past six months —

COLUMBA Anything that I can grant, Caornan.

CAORNAN I know I have no right to ask you or to expect anything. You have always been like a father to all of us here but this request I must make —

Enter GRILLAAN.

GRILLAAN The second calf was dead-born; so I have still to see twin calves.

COLUMBA Mm?

GRILLAAN The first one is quite sturdy though. And Brendan says with your permission he's going to call it Rufus.

COLUMBA A red one?

GRILLAAN Black as a raven. Did you not know? Brendan's colour blind!

COLUMBA He's not! Someone should tell him. The novices will make a terrible fool of him.

GRILLAAN Too late. They're finished in the cornfield and they're all gathered round it, stroking it and admiring it and saying it's the reddest calf they ever saw, my goodness such a red calf! And Brendan's standing there as proud as if he were the father!

They laugh. CAORNAN *rises, gathers his writing materials and prepares to leave.*

CAORNAN I think I'll do no more work today.

GRILLAAN It looks like a storm. The seagulls are settling below on the rocks.

COLUMBA It's well we got the corn cut.

CAORNAN If you'll excuse me —

COLUMBA You were asking me something, Caornan?

CAORNAN (*Confused*) Time enough, Columba. Time enough until tomorrow —

As he goes towards the door, he walks into a stool, knocks it over and stumbles.

COLUMBA Are you all right?

CAORNAN Yes — yes — yes — I'm all right — I must have
tripped on something.

> COLUMBA *holds* CAORNAN's *arm.* GRILLAAN *picks up*
> *his pen and scrolls from the floor.*

GRILLAAN Your pen, Caornan. It's broken.
CAORNAN My pen! My good pen! It was my best pen!

> COLUMBA *takes a pen from the wall.*

COLUMBA You can have mine, Caornan, the one King Brude
gave me. Here you are — a royal pen for a royal scribe.
GRILLAAN It's my opinion he broke his own deliberately. He has
always had his eye on that one.
CAORNAN (*To* COLUMBA) May I?
COLUMBA It's yours.
CAORNAN Thank you, thank you. It's a beautiful pen. Thank
you.
COLUMBA You're welcome.
CAORNAN Thank you again. Thank you —

> CAORNAN *goes off.* COLUMBA *stands looking after*
> *him.* GRILLAAN *looks at the floor where* CAORNAN
> *stumbled.*

GRILLAAN The floor is quite even.
COLUMBA I know.
GRILLAAN What are you thinking?
COLUMBA How privileged we are to live with him.

> *He turns and comes back to centre of stage.*

Do you know, Grillaan, that he wears chains which
have eaten into the flesh of his body?
GRILLAAN I am his spiritual director, too.
COLUMBA I am worried about Caornan. His sight is going and
his health is poor. I have been thinking of sending
him to Clonmore in Louth. He would be near his own
county then when the end comes.

23

GRILLAAN Strangford Lough area, isn't he?

COLUMBA Near Downpatrick. He has never once been back in Ireland in our twenty-four years here.

GRILLAAN I don't suppose he cares much.

COLUMBA He cares, Grillaan — as much as I care myself.

GRILLAAN From the day I left, thank God, Ireland never gave me a second thought.

COLUMBA He used to talk to me years ago about his father and his mother and about a sister of his that was delicate — he was very attached to her.

GRILLAAN He has got over that long ago.

COLUMBA I do know that originally he disliked Iona —

GRILLAAN Which of us liked it?

COLUMBA (*Briskly*) Anyhow remind me to speak to him tomorrow about going home.

GRILLAAN You told me to remind you about the Picts in Cromarty.

COLUMBA You're quite right. Any further news?

GRILLAAN Just what we know already: that they are supposed to be reviving old Druidical practices in the mountains there.

COLUMBA I'll go myself and find out what's happening. Very often these stories lose nothing in the telling.

GRILLAAN You'll not get away tomorrow if I'm any judge of the weather.

COLUMBA The next day then. There's nothing very urgent about it.

GRILLAAN Will you want me with you?

COLUMBA No. Diarmuid will do. We'll be gone only a few nights.

GRILLAAN (*Going to door*) He won't be keen. He says he sinks in the bogs.

COLUMBA It will take some of the beef off him. See that I'm not disturbed, will you, Grillaan? I have some prayers to catch up with.

GRILLAAN I'll see to it.

> GRILLAAN *goes off.* COLUMBA *kneels beside his bed and begins to pray. It is getting dark. Occasional gusts of wind. Pause. Then* GRILLAAN *off:*

Columba!

COLUMBA Yes?

GRILLAAN A traveller here to see you — a kinsman.

COLUMBA is irritated at being disturbed. But at the mention of kinsman, his face lights up with delight.

COLUMBA A kinsman? Bring him in! Bring him in!

Enter the messenger, BRIAN, followed by GRILLAAN. BRIAN is a young man, cool, calm, confident. He speaks quietly, never once raising his voice.

I don't know your face, kinsman, but I'll tell you something about yourself. You are from the Kingdom of O'Neill all right — from the north — just hold your chin up — that's it — yes — and you were born between two loughs, Lough Foyle and Lough Swilly, and you are an Innishowen man. Am I right?

BRIAN You are uncanny, Columba.

COLUMBA I am observant, kinsman. You are welcome to Iona.

GRILLAAN is alert, watchful, uneasy.

GRILLAAN You know one another?

COLUMBA Not his name, Grillaan, but his bones and his eyes and his neck and his shoulders and his walk. He comes from a good land; and his mother has fed him often on salmon and lobster and wild duck, and he hears Mass in Iskaheen chapel — Am I right, Innishowen man?

BRIAN You are right, Columba. My name is Brian.

COLUMBA Brian? Brian? — More likely it's your father I would know, or your grandfather. Who was he?

BRIAN You wouldn't know him, Columba, because I told you a lie. I am no kinsman of yours.

GRILLAAN I thought it strange a man appearing at this time of evening —

BRIAN I told you a lie in case you wouldn't see me. I come with a message from a kinsman.

COLUMBA Well, out with the message. Who is it from?

BRIAN From your cousin, Hugh, son of Ainmire.

COLUMBA And what's troubling big Hugh?

BRIAN It is a — (*Looks at* GRILLAAN) — a private message.

COLUMBA Grillaan, have a meal prepared for this messenger and his companions. And fix up some beds for them in the guest house, will you?

BRIAN We can't stay, Columba. Thank you all the same. We have got to return tonight. We haven't time even for a meal.

COLUMBA You're going back tonight?

BRIAN Those are Hugh's orders.

GRILLAAN You know there's a storm rising?

BRIAN Those are Hugh's orders.

COLUMBA You're not on Hugh's land now, messenger, and you take orders from me. You can risk your lives in the storm if you like but at least you'll drown on a full stomach. (*To* GRILLAAN) Tell Dochonna to get something ready.

GRILLAAN Very well, Abbot.

COLUMBA For friends, tell him, for Innishowen men.

GRILLAAN *goes off, reluctantly.*

Now Brian, what's the matter with big Hugh? He hasn't decided to get married, has he? Sit down, man, and have a rest.

GRILLAAN *is still at the door.*

What is it, Grillaan?

GRILLAAN Nothing — nothing, Abbot — nothing —

COLUMBA The best food in the house for the men of Tirconaill.

GRILLAAN *now leaves.* COLUMBA *and* BRIAN *are seated.*

Well, Brian.

BRIAN You know of Baedan's murder?

COLUMBA His father and mine were brothers. May they both

rest in peace.

BRIAN You know who murdered him?

COLUMBA He was killed by Cumine, son of Colman Beg Mac Diarmada at Léim-an-Eich.

BRIAN Nine months ago. Now that same Cumine, son of Colman Beg, and his cousin, Cumine, son of Libran, have vowed to kill Hugh —

COLUMBA *gets to his feet and begins to pace.*

COLUMBA Hugh is not an infant. He can look after himself.

BRIAN — because they see his pastures and his cattle and his horses and they have covetousness in their hearts.

COLUMBA They are all — Hugh, the two Cumines, Libran, Colman — they are all my cousins. Has Hugh forgotten that? Has he forgotten that Niall of the Nine Hostages was great-great-grandfather to all of us?

BRIAN He has not forgotten. Nor has he forgotten the Battle of Cúl-Dreimhne in the County Sligo twenty-six years ago —

COLUMBA He has a long memory, Hugh —

BRIAN — when his father fought for you against Colman's father.

COLUMBA Messenger, let me tell you a story. Once upon a time there was a monk whose father was one of the rulers of Tirconaill and whose mother was descended from the Kings of Leinster — with the result he had cousins and uncles and nephews all over the country. And every time these cousins or uncles or nephews got into a brawl — and that was very often — the first thing they said was, 'Send for our kinsman, the monk. He will settle this. He will see that *mine* is the good cause.' And invariably they sent for this monk and invariably he went because he loved them all, and maybe, too, because he was a foolish monk. Anyhow, during his life, he got himself involved in a dozen small rows and in two battles, battles in which many people were killed. But at last this monk got sense — no credit to him, messenger — because by this time he was quite old and it was as much as he could do to say his prayers and look after his communities and visit his monasteries. Before the altar of God, seven years ago, when he returned to his exile after the battle of Coleraine, he took a vow never to become embroiled in bloody conflict again. And although he has been tempted to break that vow on many occasions since, although every native instinct and inclination tore at him to go to the aid of his friends, he kept his vow — by the grace of God — for these seven years . . . . Had you a good crossing?

BRIAN *resumes as if* COLUMBA *had not spoken.*

BRIAN The Kingdom of O'Neill will never be at rest as long as Columba Beg lives.

COLUMBA We have a young novice here from Carndonagh. Perhaps you know him. His name is —

BRIAN They have three cunning leaders on their side — Colman and the two Cumines — while Hugh, your cousin, is alone.

COLUMBA His name is Kieran — he will be a fine preacher — a grand voice.

BRIAN For months they have been gathering and inciting their supporters — as far south as Fermanagh and Leitrim and Sligo — the same mob that opposed you at Cúl-Dreimhne.

COLUMBA *is getting angry — at* BRIAN'S *persistence and at his involuntary interest.*

COLUMBA A vow has been taken, messenger. With the grace of God it will be kept.

BRIAN If they are not opposed, they will sweep through Tyrone and Tirconaill and up to Derry itself. Then all the Kingdom of O'Neill will be under the tyranny of Colman and his son, the murderers of Baedan, your uncle.

COLUMBA Hugh is a wily fighter. He knows the terrain.

BRIAN He cannot fight single-handed — against God.

COLUMBA Against God?

BRIAN The priest, Sirinus, from the monastery of Bangor, is riding by the side of Colman while he musters his followers.

COLUMBA Sirinus? From Bangor?

BRIAN Comgall's monastery — the same Comgall against whom you battled at Coleraine seven years ago when Hugh stood by you like a man.

COLUMBA Comgall and I are friends now — (*There is doubt in his voice*) — and have been for the past two years — I have visited him —

BRIAN This Sirinus tells the people that Colman is leading an army to crush the irreligious Hugh, who, he says, is a sun-worshipper —

COLUMBA Rubbish!

BRIAN — and in proof of his claim, he says that Columba, the monk, hides in Iona out of shame and has denounced his cousin, Hugh, for his pagan practices.

COLUMBA That's a lie! Hugh is a good man!

BRIAN He points out that if it were not the truth, Columba, the monk, would be standing at his cousin's side, but Columba, he says, is ashamed of his cousin.

COLUMBA (*Now very angry*) That's a damned lie and you know it! I had meals with Hugh last Easter twelve months. I slept in his house. He gave me his best cow for my community here.

BRIAN Now he is alone.

COLUMBA What does Comgall say? Can he not silence this Sirinus of his?

BRIAN Comgall is at present in Aran Island, off Galway.

COLUMBA And Hugh? Hugh's no fool. Can he not speak up for himself?

BRIAN Against the word of a priest?

COLUMBA Priest? Some raving idiot who hopes to get land from Colman!

BRIAN If they are not opposed, Colman and the Cumines, they will take the land that was your father's and your grandfather's; they will drive up as far as Innish-owen. And who can tell, Columba, how your fifteen churches in these areas will fare under the mad Sirinus?

COLUMBA I will write a letter — to Hugh and to my people — to be read out to them — I will state that Hugh is a Christian and a good one — that I have never denounced him — that I am not ashamed —

BRIAN A letter is no good; they will say it is a forgery. We need a priest to lead us. They have a priest.

COLUMBA They have a liar.

BRIAN A man of God leading an army against a sun-worshipper.

COLUMBA Our Hugh is no pagan!

BRIAN They murdered Baedan last year. They will murder Hugh this year.

COLUMBA I took a vow, messenger. I told you I took a vow.

BRIAN Your fifteen churches will be in the kingdom of murderers led by a priest.

COLUMBA *switches from anger to pleading.*

COLUMBA Next Sunday is a feast day here — Finnian of Clonard — our old teacher. We — we always have a great day —

BRIAN Your own people in Gartan say, 'Columba will not disappoint us.'

COLUMBA There is a storm getting up. You could be marooned here for weeks.

BRIAN They say, 'If he loves us as he says he does, he will come.'

At the mention of Gartan, COLUMBA's *full fury is released. He catches* BRIAN *by the throat and shakes him.*

COLUMBA Listen to me, silver-tongued Innishowen man! Listen to me! I love them, yes, I love them; and every hill and stream and river and mountain from the top of Fanad down to the waters of blue Melvin. And never a day passes but I see the clouds sit down on Errigal or smell the wrack at Gweebarra or hear the wood-pigeons in the oaks of Derry. But I am a priest, messenger, a man of God, an *alter Christus* — a poor priest, but still a priest. For the sake of Christ, messenger, leave me alone! Don't wedge my frailties between my soul and its Maker!

He releases BRIAN *and goes to the far side of the stage. There is a silence.* BRIAN *is as calm as ever.* DOCHONNA *enters.*

DOCHONNA   Your meal is ready when you are.

BRIAN   What is your answer?

COLUMBA   Go and eat. You may yet be home before the storm breaks.

DOCHONNA   What's that?

COLUMBA   He's going, Dochonna. He's going now.

BRIAN   What do I say to your cousin Hugh?

DOCHONNA   This way, son. Your friends have started already.

BRIAN   We have skins in the boat to keep you warm during the crossing and there are horses waiting for us in Derry to take us the rest of the journey.

BRIAN goes off. DOCHONNA, *sensing that something is wrong, looks back at* COLUMBA.

COLUMBA   Tell Caornan I want him.

DOCHONNA   What's that, Columba?

COLUMBA   (*Irritably*) Caornan! Caornan! Tell him I need him! Now!

DOCHONNA   (*Not hearing but trying to understand*) Aye, Caornan — he's looking very poor, isn't he?

COLUMBA   (*Helplessly*) It doesn't matter — (*Waves* DOCHONNA *off*) See to the visitors, Dochonna — see to the visitors.

DOCHONNA goes off irresolutely. COLUMBA *holds his head in his hands, then goes on his knees below the crucifix and prays. After about thirty seconds* GRILLAAN *comes in.*

GRILLAAN   That fellow distinctly told me he was a relation — (*He sees* COLUMBA *praying*) I'm sorry —

COLUMBA *rises from his knees.*

What's the matter, Abbot? Bad news from home?
COLUMBA Home is a millstone round my neck, Grillaan.
GRILLAAN Something wrong in one of our houses?
COLUMBA No — no — not our houses —
GRILLAAN Thank God for that.
COLUMBA Yes. Thank God for that.

GRILLAAN *has seen this struggle before. He knows the symptoms.*

GRILLAAN Family again?
COLUMBA Again.

Pause.

GRILLAAN Columba, you are our founder, our patronus, our Abbot —
COLUMBA I know that introduction; and you are my spiritual director and you are about to lecture me —
GRILLAAN Advise you — remind you of the past — of the progress you have made in prudence and moderation —
COLUMBA Do you know what Colman Beg is saying? That Hugh, big, innocent, guileless, thick-headed, quick-tempered Hugh is a sun-worshipper! Hugh!
GRILLAAN And he wants you to bless his men and pray over them and dignify his brawl with a crucifix?
COLUMBA Our churches in Tyrone and Tirconaill are in danger.
GRILLAAN They always are.
COLUMBA I mean it, Grillaan.
GRILLAAN And his enemies — whoever they are this time — no doubt they have a churchman to bless their standards too, with the result that God is fighting for both causes. Isn't that the usual pattern?
COLUMBA A mad monk leading a gang of murderers!
GRILLAAN You are a priest — not a rallying cry!
COLUMBA (*Controlled*) Hugh is my cousin and a good man. We ate his barley bread for lunch today. It was his cow that calved in the meadow today.

Both tempers are now up. The two monks raise their voices.

GRILLAAN And this is the payment he demands? That you kneel bare-headed on a hill-top, an old man with white hair, Columba the church-builder, and pray aloud for victory for the drunken land-grabbers fighting below your feet?

COLUMBA Easy, Prior, easy!

GRILLAAN Have you a better name for them? Do you absolve them before they reel into battle, their beery faces flushed with blood lust, or do you wait until 'right' has conquered and give the dead of both sides conditional absolution?

COLUMBA We come of kings, Prior. To lead is in our blood. We are not savages.

GRILLAAN You are a priest — with a priest's vows.

COLUMBA Royal blood that answers to the call of its people! Kings of Leinster and rulers of the land of Conall!

GRILLAAN (*Changing tactics*) Columba, listen to me, listen. You are a holy man, Columba. You haven't eaten a proper meal since we came to this place; you haven't slept for more than five hours any night. You pray longer and harder than any of us do. You do the most menial jobs in the monastery —

COLUMBA Please, Grillaan, please —

GRILLAAN You are kind and humble and generous and self-sacrificing and God has blessed your work a hundred, thousand fold. Everything, Columba, everything you have surrendered but this one. And now is your opportunity.

BRIAN appears suddenly at the door.

BRIAN There is not time to eat. Let us get away before the wind rises.

He comes into the room. COLUMBA is in the centre, GRILLAAN on one side of him, BRIAN on the other. He is torn between the two.

33

GRILLAAN The last tie, Columba. Cut it now. Cut it. Cut it.

BRIAN They are your people. It is your land.

GRILLAAN A priest or a politician — which?

BRIAN They rallied round you at Sligo and at Coleraine. All they ask is your blessing.

GRILLAAN He that loveth father or mother more than Me is not worthy of Me.

BRIAN Are they to die in their sins at the hands of murderers?

GRILLAAN You are a priest in voluntary exile for God — not a private chaplain to your family.

BRIAN Son of Fedhlimidh and Eithne.

GRILLAAN Abbot!

> COLUMBA *has been standing absolutely motionless. Now as if he were demented, he comes alive, strides to the door and roars:*

COLUMBA Diarmuid! Diarmuid!

> GRILLAAN *knows that he has lost.* COLUMBA *knows he cannot afford to listen to him. He charges around the stage, barking instructions, gathering his belongings, consciously busying himself. He avoids* GRILLAAN's *eyes.*

Hoist your sails, Innishowen man, and strip your oarsmen to the waist! Hurry! Hurry! (BRIAN *goes off.* COLUMBA *turns to* GRILLAAN) You will be in charge, Prior, until I return. Travel to Cromarty tomorrow — take Cormac with you — and find out what's brewing there. And on Sunday see that the feast's a worthy one.

> DIARMUID — *puffing* — *enters.*

DIARMUID Yes, Columba?

COLUMBA Get into your travelling clothes! We are going home! Now!

> DIARMUID *stands aghast. He might even consider*

34

trying to joke his way out of another sea journey.

Are you deaf too? What have I here? A nunnery of
senile crones?

DIARMUID My stomach, Columba —

COLUMBA At once, I say, monk! Obedience!

> DIARMUID *goes off quickly.* COLUMBA's *fury dies
> suddenly.* GRILLAAN *is standing far off from him with
> his back to him. He looks at* GRILLAAN's *back, hangs
> his head and slowly — very slowly — goes towards
> him. Then he kneels behind the Prior.*

(*Softly*) Grillaan, your blessing.

> GRILLAAN *does not move. Pause.*

(*Slightly louder*) Your blessing, Grillaan.

> OSWALD *stands framed in the door.*

(*Still louder*) Grillaan — ?

> *He looks up at* GRILLAAN, *sees the hard back to him,
> waits for five seconds, then, his fury roused again, he
> jumps to his feet and charges towards the door. As*
> COLUMBA *comes towards him,* OSWALD *says:*

OSWALD You said you would talk to me after I had eaten,
Columba —

> COLUMBA *scarcely sees him. He brushes roughly past
> him, knocking him to the side as he goes out.* OSWALD
> *looks towards* GRILLAAN's *back, questioningly. What
> has he done wrong, his look asks. Then* GRILLAAN
> *turns round slowly and looks beyond* OSWALD *to the
> door. Now the storm breaks — thunder, lightning,
> wind — a tremendous crash.*
> *Quick curtain.*

ACT TWO

Scene One

There is an air of happy anticipation: COLUMBA *is home again; he is getting out of the boat at the harbour below.* GRILLAAN *is taking the straw off Columba's bed and putting things in order. He is happy but he hides his pleasure in working.* DOCHONNA *is standing at the door from where he can see the harbour. He reports to* GRILLAAN *all that is happening. He is beaming with joy and bouncing up and down on his toes in jerky, restless movements. Occasionally he breaks into a high-pitched giggle.*

DOCHONNA   They have pulled her on the slip now and they're carrying stuff off her. And — aye — aye — aye — it's Diarmuid — it's Diarmuid all right — lying across the wall of the pier and vomiting his stomach out — (*Giggles*)

         BRENDAN *enters, carrying an armful of fresh straw.*

         Get a move on, boy. He'll be here in a minute or two.

GRILLAAN   (*To* DOCHONNA) Have you a meal ready for them? (*To* BRENDAN) Just throw it there. (*To* DOCHONNA) Have you a meal ready?

DOCHONNA   What's that?

GRILLAAN   Food. Have you food?

DOCHONNA   Aye, aye. Aye. Food. In the oven. Waiting.

GRILLAAN   (*To* BRENDAN) Take this straw away and clean up the floor.

DOCHONNA   He's saying goodbye to the boatman. They mustn't be coming up.

BRENDAN   (*To* GRILLAAN) Are you going to tell him this evening?

GRILLAAN   I've got to. He's bound to ask.

DOCHONNA   (*Laughs*) Diarmuid — he's pulled himself away from the wall and he's reeling up the path — and his face — it's the colour of pea soup —

> BRENDAN *goes off with the old straw.*

He's coming now himself — he's coming — he's coming —

> DOCHONNA *comes into the room and begins fussing about.*

GRILLAAN   Shove that table over to the corner and clean up the floor.

DOCHONNA   (*Not hearing*) The place feels different already, doesn't it, eh? Like — it's full again, isn't it?

GRILLAAN   Bring the food in now. On a tray. The food.

DOCHONNA   Oh, aye, aye, the food —

> He goes towards the door, singing: 'The Abbot's back, the Abbot's back, the Abbot's back to Iona' —

GRILLAAN   Dochonna!

DOCHONNA   Eh? Eh? What? What?

GRILLAAN   I'll break the news to him — later on.

> DOCHONNA *looks blankly at him.*

About Caornan. We'll wait until he has settled in.

DOCHONNA   (*Suddenly very old, dejected*) Caornan — aye — Caornan —

> He shuffles out — an old, old man — mumbling 'Caornan . . . Caornan'. GRILLAAN *goes on working. Then* BRENDAN *returns.*

BRENDAN   Diarmuid's outside and Columba's half-way up the path.

GRILLAAN   I'm telling Dochonna — we'll wait until he has settled in and has something to eat.

37

BRENDAN   He's going to take it badly.

GRILLAAN   I know, I know. We'll give him the best welcome we can.

BRENDAN   Maybe you shouldn't tell him until tomorrow?

GRILLAAN   Caornan will be the first he'll ask for.

> *Enter* DIARMUID — *staggering* — *groaning. He has been sick during the crossing and is determined to make everybody aware of his reduced condition.*

DIARMUID   Awwwwww — !

> *He reels across the stage and drops onto the bed.*

GRILLAAN   Diarmuid! How are you, man? How are you?

BRENDAN   (*Solemnly*) Awwwwww — !

GRILLAAN   What sort of crossing had you?

DIARMUID   Crabs — in the bottom of the boat — I was going great until I smelt them —

BRENDAN   Was Columba sick too?

DIARMUID   All he could do was laugh — aw, those boats — they'll kill me yet —

GRILLAAN   Was there much bloodshed over there?

DIARMUID   Please — please —

> DOCHONNA — *happy again* — *comes in with a tray.*

DOCHONNA   He made it, did he? Good man yourself, Diarmuid —

DIARMUID   (*Faintest greeting*) Dochonna —

DOCHONNA   You're ravenous, are you, eh? Look what I have here for you — mutton chops — just what you love!

> DIARMUID *groans even louder and covers his eyes.*

GRILLAAN   (*To* DOCHONNA) Seasick.

DOCHONNA   But this is good for him. Something to get up again.

GRILLAAN   Let him be. Let him be. Listen!

COLUMBA   (*Off*) And it's good to see you, too. Yes — yes — I'll be over later — later.

BRENDAN   It's himself!

COLUMBA (*Off*) I've got a new skin for the currach. I'll bring it over later. Right — right —

GRILLAAN Remember — not a word until he has eaten!

> COLUMBA *enters. He is loaded with wooden boxes of all sizes. As with his entrance in Act One he seems to charge the atmosphere with vigour and vitality. He is delighted at being back. The three monks gather round him;* DOCHONNA *almost frisking with joy at having the Abbot home again.*

COLUMBA Grillaan! And Dochonna! And Brendan! It's good to see you.

DOCHONNA Welcome home, Columba! Welcome! Welcome!

GRILLAAN The change did you good.

COLUMBA Good? I feel as fresh as a novice, Grillaan. And Dochonna? How are you, Dochonna!

> *The emotional stress — Caornan's death, the Abbot's return — is too much for the old man. He holds on to* COLUMBA's *arm and begins to cry.*

DOCHONNA Don't go away again, Columba. Don't leave us.

COLUMBA (*Pause — then briskly*) Here man, what sort of a welcome is this? Three weeks — that's all I was gone. And wait until you see what I've got for you here — and something for Caornan —

> DIARMUID *groans —* COLUMBA *starts.*

Is he — ? (*Sees that it is* DIARMUID) Oh, it's only the sailor. I thought for a moment —

GRILLAAN (*Quickly*) You must be hungry, Columba. Dochonna has a meal here for you.

COLUMBA Later. Later. But the news first! How did you get on without me?

BRENDAN We got the last of the hay in today.

COLUMBA How's the calf doing, Brendan?

BRENDAN Thriving, Columba.

COLUMBA I've got something here for you, too.

39

He begins rooting through his boxes.

GRILLAAN Was there a battle, Columba?

COLUMBA Battle? No. There was no battle because the rats wouldn't stand for a battle. Ran like the hammers of Jericho down through Monaghan and Cavan and when we cornered them at a place called Cúl-Fheadha on the banks of the Blackwater — Diarmuid can tell you — if they had half a hundred scamps behind them, that was the height of it. And Sirinus, the monk — we had a good name for him; we called him 'The Brave Beetle' because he was a black wart of a man. Led the retreat as hard as he could go! But a monk? He was no monk, yon fellow! Comgall himself never heard of him!

GRILLAAN Were many killed?

Pause.

COLUMBA (*Quietly*) Colman Beg, son of Diarmuid, and Libran, son of Illadhan, and a dozen or so slaves. God rest their souls.

GRILLAAN And Hugh?

COLUMBA (*Elated*) Hugh's married. The day before yesterday! In the Raphoe church!

GRILLAAN No!

COLUMBA We would have been back last Friday but for that. To a girl from near Aughnacloy. A fine girl she is, too. He saw her for the first time on our way south when we were chasing the MacDiarmuid mob and on the way home — not a whisper to any of us — didn't he take her back with him! You should have seen my face when he said to me, 'Columba, will you do a wee job for me?'

GRILLAAN Good for Hugh.

COLUMBA They've been eating and drinking there for the past ten days. Don't think it was the crossing alone that set the sailor here off!

DOCHONNA You weren't over by the west in your travels, were you?

40

COLUMBA Where were we anyhow? We were in Derry and Kilmacrenan and Gartan and Raphoe for Hugh's wedding — when was that?

GRILLAAN That would be last Tuesday.

COLUMBA Tuesday — and the Saturday before that we were in Kilmore. They had the new chapel finished there now — a beautiful job. And Fedhlimidh himself was asking for you all. He wanted us to go to Kells with him the following day but we were anxious to get back. And then on the Monday we had lunch in Ballymagroarty and that night we stayed in Ballynascreen. I think that was everywhere. No, a night with Comgall in Bangor!

GRILLAAN How are they all in Derry?

COLUMBA Do you know who I met there? Old Fintan!

GRILLAAN (*Parodying the Cork accent*) Fintan from Cork?

COLUMBA No, not that Fintan. Do you remember a very tall lanky man in Clonard? Do you not remember they used to pull his leg about being able to reach up to the bell tower to ring the bell! (*To* DOCHONNA) You would remember him, Dochonna. Fintan — big, long Fintan.

DOCHONNA Fintan, eh? Fintan Caol?

COLUMBA Fintan Caol! The very name!

DOCHONNA You met him again. How is he? He must be a right age now, eh?

COLUMBA Ninety-six, he tells me.

DOCHONNA And going strong?

COLUMBA Like a boy.

DOCHONNA (*Looking around*) There now! And he could be my father!

COLUMBA As straight as a rush and as clear in the head as Brendan there. He gave me a present of a pen for Caornan because he said he never saw work to equal his in all his days. Where *is* Caornan? Go and tell him I'm back, Brendan.

> BRENDAN *looks at* GRILLAAN. GRILLAAN *signals to him to stay where he is.*

GRILLAAN What have you got in all these parcels?

COLUMBA What have I not got? The boat couldn't hold half the stuff Hugh gave us. What have we anyhow? (*Opening boxes*) Candles for the chapel from Comgall —

DOCHONNA (*Picking up the word*) Comgall, aye, that's Comgall of Bangor.

COLUMBA Talking fourteen to the dozen as usual. And a crate of honey from Hugh. And what's this? Yes, yes, a crucifix from the Derry house. The best of oak. And a side of bacon from Hugh too —

GRILLAAN We'll not starve this winter.

COLUMBA And for you, Grillaan — a present. (*Holds up a pair of sandals*) I heard you sniffing a lot before I left.

GRILLAAN That was the haymaking did that.

COLUMBA If they don't fit, we can get them changed.

GRILLAAN Sandals! Beautiful soft sandals!

BRENDAN The novices will never hear you coming in those!

GRILLAAN Thanks, Columba. The very thing I needed.

> *He takes them to the other side of the stage to try them on. During the distribution of these presents, there is a childlike simplicity and joy in the giving and receiving.*

COLUMBA And Dochonna — something for your hearing.

DOCHONNA What's that, Columba, eh?

COLUMBA A tip an old fellow in Raphoe gave me — for your hearing.

> *He produces the horn of a cow.*

DOCHONNA What — what is it?

COLUMBA It's the horn of a cow. When anyone wishes to speak to you, he speaks through this end here.

> DOCHONNA *takes it and puts it up on his temple.*

DOCHONNA Eh? Eh? Like this here? Eh?

BRENDAN He's like the leader of the Vandals! Look, Grillaan.

COLUMBA No, no, no, no. This way. The small end *into* your ear.

DOCHONNA Aye?

COLUMBA You hold it there and I speak through here.

DOCHONNA (*Very pleased*) I hear — I hear the water of Lough
Conn —

BRENDAN He thinks it's a sea shell.

COLUMBA (*Speaking into horn*) Does it sound better?

DOCHONNA Aye, water. That's what I'm telling you. Water — like
home —

He wanders away smiling to himself. GRILLAAN *struts
across the stage with mock elegance, holding his habit
up to his knees.*

GRILLAAN Well?

COLUMBA Are they comfortable?

GRILLAAN As fur.

COLUMBA Good. I took the biggest pair I could get.

GRILLAAN Your own aren't so small.

COLUMBA And Brendan — for the calf — a curry comb.

BRENDAN That was very thoughtful of you, Columba.

COLUMBA With a black handle to match his coat.

BRENDAN The calf is red — but that doesn't matter.

COLUMBA Stupid me! It was the black one that died, wasn't it?

BRENDAN It was white, Columba.

COLUMBA *sees* GRILLAAN *laughing at him.*

COLUMBA Huh! Well — whatever colour it was —

BRENDAN Thank you again.

COLUMBA And now — Caornan. What's keeping him? Did you
tell him I had come?

GRILLAAN The meat is getting cold, Columba. What about some-
thing to eat now?

COLUMBA *suddenly senses that something is wrong.*

COLUMBA Where is Caornan? Caornan, where is he?

BRENDAN *and* GRILLAAN *look away.* DIARMUID *sits
upright on the bed.*

Brendan — Grillaan — where is Caornan, the scholar?

There is a pause. Then suddenly COLUMBA *impetuously goes to the door and roars:*

Caor-nan!

GRILLAAN It happened within twenty-four hours after you left —

COLUMBA (*Slightly softer*) Caor-nan!

GRILLAAN That night he got up in the small hours, as he always did, for his vigil. There was a high wind and no moon. We believe he tripped on a stone and struck his head on the old anvil at the door of the forge.

DIARMUID Dead?

COLUMBA (*Whisper*) Caor-nan —

GRILLAAN Brendan found him at dawn. He was alive then and conscious until he died a few hours later. He asked me to thank you for all your kindness to him. He said he would not forget you.

Enter DOCHONNA.

DIARMUID He is with God now because he was a simple man.

GRILLAAN He spoke to each of us in turn — he lay there on your bed; this was the nearest room — but to Dochonna most of all. And although he spoke in a whisper, he heard every word he said. Then he got the Eucharist. Then he died.

DIARMUID What day was that?

GRILLAAN It was Thursday.

DIARMUID We were in Kilmacrenan on Thursday — feasting before the battle.

COLUMBA *is standing looking down at his bed.*

GRILLAAN We thought of sending for you — Brendan volunteered to go and find you — but we had no idea where to look. You could have been in any of fifty places!

DIARMUID That's where we were. Singing and feasting and laughing.

COLUMBA Caornan, son of regal Ronan and the fair Maeve, clean child of Down with the wisdom of twelve men, monk and true man of God, my Caornan, my brother Caornan —

He buries his face in his hands and sobs.

GRILLAAN We buried him with his chains. They were part of the body in places.

DIARMUID (*To* DOCHONNA) What were his last words?

GRILLAAN He spoke to the novices and to the deacons and then to the monks —

COLUMBA I had a surprise for Caornan — to be kept secret until next week.

DIARMUID He arranged for him to have a large, well-lit room in the Clonmore house, a stone's throw from his birthplace. The boat was to call for him next Wednesday.

COLUMBA The day I left he said he had a request to make — I knew what it was: because of his health and years, to release him from his exile and allow him to die in Ireland — a big room and a big table and a small chair — they are waiting for him.

DIARMUID What did he say to you, Dochonna?

DOCHONNA Caornan?

DIARMUID His last words to you.

DOCHONNA He said — he said that if God should spare him, he was going to ask the Abbot to release him because he said that as the years had gone by, he had come to love Iona and he was too happy here with all his own friends. So he was going to ask the Abbot to let him go up to the Isles of Orkney and find a hermitage there —

COLUMBA Orkney?

DOCHONNA For there he would be all alone and there he could do penance for all the joy he found in the life here. And — and — and —

DOCHONNA *goes to* COLUMBA *and holds on to him.*

45

— and he called me 'The Hardy Trout' —

He breaks down. COLUMBA *and he hold on to one another.*

COLUMBA The old doter was five years older than me — that's one thing he could never deny — the old doter — They call me Sanctus, Sanctus Pater, Sanctus Senior — Merciful Christ, give me the sight of Caornan, your scribe. Have pity on me.

Quick curtain.

ACT TWO

Scene Two

Later that day. COLUMBA *and* GRILLAAN *are seated at the table looking at a map.* COLUMBA *is very quiet, as if he were preoccupied.* GRILLAAN, *knowing this, talks on and on in the hope of interesting him.*

GRILLAAN   We spent the first night in the north of Argyll and the following day we travelled along the banks of Lough Ness and slept that night in a shepherd's hut. The next night we crossed into Cromarty — somewhere around here — Cormac and the guide and myself.

COLUMBA   Guide?

GRILLAAN   I told you. We called with Gregory in Bracholy on the second day. He insisted we take a guide with us.

COLUMBA   Yes — yes — yes —

GRILLAAN   So we worked our way up the coast here — and right across the plain between Ben Wyvis and the sea. Then we doubled back, crossed into Inverness again, travelling this time down along the northern bank of the lough. The guide came with us all the way. (*Pauses for* COLUMBA *to comment*) We discovered very little — apart from the fact that Druidism is as good as dead. The stories we heard were completely false. Not a trace of an organized revival. We did discover though that many families that had been Christian ten or fifteen years ago have fallen away because they never see a priest from one year to the next. (*He looks at* COLUMBA *to see if he is showing any interest*) You have no idea how isolated some of those houses are. We even came across one old fellow who thought we were Romans! And Rome, he thought was one of the

Shetland Islands. That sort of thing —

COLUMBA So there is no fear of a rebirth of Druidism.

He rises from the table and walks across the stage. GRILLAAN *looks after him and then goes on talking.*

GRILLAAN Gregory had some interesting stories. He was telling us about a young German who arrived at his monastery one night in the middle of last winter. They hadn't seen a soul for weeks — completely cut off with snow drifts — when suddenly this night, as they were about to retire, there was a gentle tapping on the door. He must have been leaning against the door because when it was pulled back, he fell into the room. They lifted him up and carried him to a bed. Gregory said that he mustn't have had a bite to eat for at least a week. Anyhow they heard this story. His great-grandfather, he claimed, was helmsman on board the ship that brought Patrick back to Ireland with the faith. And —

COLUMBA *interrupts him. He has not heard a word that* GRILLAAN *has said.*

COLUMBA Grillaan, I want you, as my spiritual adviser, to impose on me the most severe penances you can think of: starvation, beating, weeks of unceasing prayer — anything, all of them, whatever you advise.

GRILLAAN I have advised you before, Columba.

COLUMBA I know. I know. Prudence, you say, and patience, and counsel — the virtues of old men with wet chins and shapeless feet. But I cannot *feel* my sixty-six years, Grillaan. I am burdened with this strong, active body that responds to the whistle of movement, the fight of the sail, the swing of the axe, the warm breadth of a horse beneath it, the challenge of a new territory. I try! I try! And it betrays me!

GRILLAAN We have talked of this often, Columba.

COLUMBA Let me fast. Give me Caornan's chains. Forbid me my bed for five years. But conquer me, Grillaan! Crush this violent Adam into subjection!

GRILLAAN I need your full obedience — your willing obedience.

COLUMBA You have it. You know that.

GRILLAAN To do exactly — *exactly* as I say.

COLUMBA Exactly, with God's grace.

GRILLAAN I believe your course is simple. You must live the Rule of Iona to the letter.

COLUMBA I try to —

GRILLAAN No. You exceed it, Columba. You eat less each day than a sparrow eats. You sleep only three hours at night. You pray longer and work harder than anyone else in the island. And those very excesses are surrenderings to this Adam you speak of.

COLUMBA Excesses?

GRILLAAN Columba, may I, the least worthy, advise you?

COLUMBA Whatever you say, I will do it.

GRILLAAN I say to you: subject yourself to the wise discipline of the monastery and to it alone; eat your two meals a day; sleep your five hours sleep; read your Office; celebrate your Mass; look after your administrative work. And beyond that — nothing. No more immersions in icy water, no more fasts or vigils or days of prayer. Only the Rule — but the Rule to the letter. Each man's cleansing, Columba, is of a different kind. Yours is in moderation in all things, in calm, reasoned moderation. This I advise.

COLUMBA And atonement for my past?

GRILLAAN In some men, Abbot — as it was with Caornan — sanctity is a progression, a building of stone upon stone, year after year, until the edifice is complete. In other men, it is in the will and determination to start, and then to start again, and then to start again, so that their life is a series of beginnings. You are of the second kind, Columba.

COLUMBA So I must begin again — like a novice!

GRILLAAN The Rule is a wise rule.

COLUMBA But at times when I need to do penance for all my violence —

GRILLAAN Your greatest penance will be found in keeping the Rule.

COLUMBA At sixty-six I am back where I began! It is a poor record!

GRILLAAN You will take my guidance?

COLUMBA With God's help, Grillaan. I am no leader for you.

GRILLAAN We need no leader — but a father. And that we have. (*Changing the subject*) You told me nothing about the battle yet, Columba.

COLUMBA It was no battle. I told you that. A shabby squabble between neighbours. I stood on a hill, as you said I would, prudent Grillaan, and watched them below me, hack at each other.

GRILLAAN It's never any different.

COLUMBA Never again — no, never — I know I've said that before, dozens of times. But there on the banks of the Blackwater, I saw Colman Beg being split and fall from his horse. Although he was my enemy, I ran as fast as I could. But when I got to him, he was dead, his white hair loose about the grass, his eyes open, his strong face calm and at peace. (*Pause*) He had a look of my father, Grillaan.

GRILLAAN (*Still trying to brighten him*) And Hugh is married! After all these years.

OSWALD *appears at the door. Stands there.*

COLUMBA Time for him, too.

GRILLAAN The honey is very sweet. Brendan says his bees are put to shame.

COLUMBA (*To himself*) Prudence — that's what I need — and calm, reasoned moderation.

Now GRILLAAN *sees* OSWALD *at the door.*

GRILLAAN Oswald! Come in, boy! Come in!

COLUMBA Yes — the young Englishman, isn't it?

OSWALD I wish to speak to you, Columba.

COLUMBA By all means, Oswald. Come on in.

GRILLAAN I was about to leave anyhow.

OSWALD *enters room.* GRILLAAN *goes to door.*

COLUMBA Thank you, Grillaan. What was it you called it? — The will and determination to begin? It's there — it's there in plenty.

> GRILLAAN *smiles back. Then leaves.* OSWALD *enters. He has the same intense look as when we first saw him. It is clear that* COLUMBA *is a hero to him: he never takes his eyes off him. His body, his movements, his voice are stilled and hushed in the Abbot's presence.* COLUMBA — *the man of action* — *is not aware of this. He brightens considerably when* OSWALD *comes in.*

Now, Oswald, the Englishman, how does Iona suit you? Pull up a stool there and sit down.

OSWALD You have been gone twenty-two days.

COLUMBA And now I'm back again to start — with you. You and I together, Oswald. Are you happy here?

OSWALD I am now, for the first time.

COLUMBA Every novice is homesick. It's nothing to be ashamed of — provided it still isn't tugging at him when he's an old man.

OSWALD I've never been so miserable in all my life.

COLUMBA They tell me the South of England is a beautiful place.

OSWALD I wasn't homesick, Abbot. Five minutes after I had left home, I forgot what it looked like.

COLUMBA You are lucky then, young Oswald. Detachment is a precious thing. How are you getting on with the other novices?

OSWALD I hate them! I hate every single one of them! I dread the hours when we are permitted to talk!

COLUMBA No, no, you don't hate —

OSWALD Great, rustic louts who mock my accent and my table manners and the way I pronounce the Latin —

COLUMBA Your ways are new to them.

OSWALD And their endless joking and camaraderie and coarse humour so that if you make a serious comment, they pounce on it and turn it to ridicule.

COLUMBA That is something you will discover always where men are cut off from the refining influence of women, Oswald. The same with soldiers, the same with

	sailors. I wouldn't let it upset me. Be — yes, be prudent in your judgement of them.
OSWALD	I can forget about them now that you're back. They don't exist any more.
COLUMBA	Tell me, Oswald, why did you choose Iona?
OSWALD	Why?
COLUMBA	When Aidan wrote to me to ask me to accept you, he spoke so highly of you that I wondered at the time he hadn't persuaded you to join his own monastery.
OSWALD	He did try.
COLUMBA	And you preferred to come here?
OSWALD	Yes.
COLUMBA	I believe you were wise. It is not a good thing to be near home, Oswald.
OSWALD	That did not influence me.
COLUMBA	What did, then?

From here on, OSWALD is unable to contain himself. His boyish hero-worship of COLUMBA must be spoken. At first COLUMBA does not understand, is then amused, then irritated, finally — because of his own sense of guilt — infuriated.

OSWALD	You. I had to be with you.
COLUMBA	Me?
OSWALD	(*In a rush*) Everybody in the South of England knows of you and talks of you. From I was so high, when I first heard of you, I knew that one day I would join you here in Iona. I have always admired you more than anybody else in my whole life.
COLUMBA	'In your whole life!' Oswald, son, God has many strange ways of calling each of us. But we must not confuse the means with the end. You are here only because you wish above all things to be a monk.
OSWALD	And to be with you, to see you, to watch you, to copy you, to do everything exactly as you do it.
COLUMBA	Hold on! Hold on! Hold on! You are young, Oswald, and inexperienced —
OSWALD	You eat practically nothing and you sleep only three hours each night —

COLUMBA (*Calmly*) Will you listen to me?

OSWALD Sorry.

COLUMBA Young boys need heroes, Oswald. When I was your age, our hero was Niall of the Nine Hostages. We used to play Niall day in and day out; and we used to fight among ourselves who would be leader next, because each of us wanted to be Niall the King and none of us wanted to be the leader of the enemy. Then as I grew older I learned some things about Niall — that he was pig-headed, and blustering, and blood-thirsty, and his temper was violent, and he was a very, very imprudent ruler of his people.

OSWALD You have prophesied the future many times and —

COLUMBA In the same way, Oswald, you, too, may have had an idea of a man, built out of old women's tales and endowed with every possible virtue by simple pious folk. But you are not a child now —

OSWALD You have changed water into wine, and cast out devils, and calmed a stormy sea, and spoken with the angels —

COLUMBA (*Angrily*) You are not a child, I say. You are a man — or at least the makings of a man. (*Calm again*) Now, Oswald, now together, you and I, we are going to try to become holy men because that is why we are here. Together we will start. And the first thing we have got to do is to keep the Rule of the monastery. At this moment you should be at your Scripture lessons and I should be in the chapel.

OSWALD You raised a boy from the dead. He was lying in his coffin and before dozens of witnesses you stretched out your hand —

COLUMBA And you must remember that I am Abbot here — to be obeyed.

OSWALD You knew when Finnian of Clonard died. You had a vision in the church in Derry. You must have known, too, when the old blind man here had died.

COLUMBA Get to your Scripture lesson.

OSWALD You knew he was dead. You had a vision over in Ireland. An angel told you. You are too humble to speak about it.

COLUMBA Get out of my way, boy! I am trying to start again!

OSWALD The others may say that you are too stern or too lenient or too mild or too quick; but I know the wonderful man you are, the man of heroic virtue —

COLUMBA Stop it! Stop it! Stop it!

OSWALD Because I know that you are a saint, Columba!

> COLUMBA *slaps him across the face with his open hand.* OSWALD *looks at him in shock, in horror. Then turns and runs off.* COLUMBA *pauses for a second, trying to realise what he has done. Then he rushes to the door calling:*

COLUMBA Oswald — Oswald — I'm sorry, Oswald — come back — come back — Oh God, I'm sorry —

> *Curtain.*

ACT THREE

DIARMUID *is working at the table where* CAORNAN *used to work. When he dips his pen into the ink, which he keeps on the floor, he turns his face away so that he will not smell the ink.* BRENDAN *enters. He moves wearily. He is carrying a cloak.*

DIARMUID Any luck?

BRENDAN *shakes his head.*

BRENDAN Where will I leave this?
DIARMUID Throw it on the bed there.

BRENDAN *leaves the cloak on the bed.*

You're wasting your time. He has cleared off to the South of England. What does he say himself?
BRENDAN Nothing.
DIARMUID And I suppose he went straight from the boat to the chapel?

BRENDAN *nods: Yes.*

All over a young, conceited brat of a novice! That was my opinion of him. A pup!
BRENDAN Everywhere we go, he stumbles over the heather and through the rocks, calling 'Oswald — Oswald' as if it were his own child he was looking for.
DIARMUID Where were you today?
BRENDAN North end of Mull.
DIARMUID He's gone. Told him that myself. At this moment he's sitting in Daddy's best armchair and making his posh friends chuckle at his little escapade — three weeks on an island monastery.

55

BRENDAN How's it going?

DIARMUID Rotten!

BRENDAN Mm. Mm. Mm. Fair. A bit spidery — but — quite good, everything considered.

DIARMUID It's very good.

BRENDAN That's what I say — apart from those smudges there — and the unevenness of the lines —

DIARMUID What lines?

BRENDAN Those and those. And those and those.

DIARMUID *looks more closely at the work.*

DIARMUID The ink is the cause of that.

BRENDAN And the pen and the rough table and the poor quality of the paper.

DIARMUID Not the ink itself but the smell of it. It goes for me here. (*He indicates his stomach.* BRENDAN *pretends to be very sympathetic*)

BRENDAN Where?

DIARMUID Here. Just there.

BRENDAN Tch, tch.

DIARMUID That's why I have to keep it on the floor. And every time I need a dip, I have to do it behind my back! That's why I have so little done.

BRENDAN Yes. Very awkward. Tch, tch.

DIARMUID Even if I hold it at my side — like this here — the very sight of the thing sets me off.

BRENDAN I know.

DIARMUID And if I get a whiff of the ink itself — Ohhhhhhhh! The searing pain shoots right up to the chest.

BRENDAN I wonder — still, no —

DIARMUID What?

BRENDAN I was going to suggest that you leave the inkwell outside the door altogether.

DIARMUID Eh?

BRENDAN Then you would neither see it nor smell it.

DIARMUID You may laugh! It's easily seen you were never doubled up with excruciating agonies!

BRENDAN *moves away laughing.*

BRENDAN   You have no one to thank but yourself, Diarmuid. What have you tried so far? Sacristan, cook, smithy, carpenter, weaver, mason, silversmith, novice-master, personal attendant to the Abbot, and now scribe. No wonder we call you our 'all round' man!

DIARMUID   When I was sacristan, it was the candles; when I was cook, it was the smell of fat; when I was smithy, it was the heat of the furnace; when I was —

BRENDAN   I'm not criticising you, Diarmuid. I'm just pointing out that this is the only job you hadn't tried. If you ask me, he's been more than patient with you.

DIARMUID   Brendan, I — I'm thinking of asking for another change.

BRENDAN   But you've been round them all!

DIARMUID   My old job back — I've been thinking about it here.

BRENDAN   Which of the ten, Diarmuid?

DIARMUID   Yours.

BRENDAN   Mine?

DIARMUID   You would like to get back to the farming again, wouldn't you?

BRENDAN   But your stomach and the boats and all the travelling —

DIARMUID   I have it all worked out. I'll wait until he gives up this mad search of his. It will soon be winter. He has been in Ireland a month ago so he won't be going there for a long time. He isn't due a visit to the Scottish houses for another nine months. And even if an emergency should arise, it would probably be too stormy to go anywhere.

BRENDAN   You're a crafty old fox!

DIARMUID   It's not for myself, Brendan, you know that. It's for my stomach.

BRENDAN   Of course, Diarmuid.

DIARMUID   A good plan, eh?

BRENDAN   Very good.

DIARMUID   You don't mind being shifted around?

BRENDAN   As long as it's for the good of your health.

DIARMUID   Good man. I knew you would understand. Now you run along and get something to eat. I suppose you had nothing since yesterday.

BRENDAN	A slice of bread.
DIARMUID	Tch, tch, tch. That's the way I used to be — completely indifferent to myself. And now look at me. What I mean is, now I just have to take care of myself if I'm not to be a dead weight on the community.
BRENDAN	Dochonna will scrape up something for me.
DIARMUID	Poor Dochonna. Have you noticed, Brendan?
BRENDAN	I have.
DIARMUID	It must have been the shock of Caornan's death.
BRENDAN	He seems happy enough, though.
DIARMUID	Living in the past.

BRENDAN *is about to go off.*

BRENDAN	Tell him his cloak's over there.
DIARMUID	We had new roots today. Very nice they were, too.
BRENDAN	I dug them this morning before we left.
DIARMUID	Yes, I think I'll join you — I always find that I can work much better after a little break.

DIARMUID *rises from the table and joins* BRENDAN.

BRENDAN	Too much concentration is bad for the stomach.
DIARMUID	You find that too? Exactly the same with me. Concentration and long fasts — disastrous! The best cure I know is small quantities of food frequently —

At the door they meet GRILLAAN *coming in.* DIARMUID *stands in the doorway.*

GRILLAAN	The Abbot's not here?
BRENDAN	He's around somewhere. Did you try the chapel?
GRILLAAN	I've just been there.
DIARMUID	Here he is.
BRENDAN	His clothes are wet. You should persuade him to change.
GRILLAAN	Persuade *him*?

COLUMBA *enters. For the first time he looks his years. Tired, weary, apathetic. His face is drawn and worried.*

At last he is old. On his way past DIARMUID *he pats him on the shoulder and says, 'Well, Diarmuid' and crosses the stage and drops into a seat.*

BRENDAN Did you leave the rowlocks in the boat, Columba?
COLUMBA I did. We'll be needing them again tomorrow.
BRENDAN Right. Give me a call when you need me.
DIARMUID Thank you, Brendan. Thank you.

> BRENDAN *and* DIARMUID *go off.* GRILLAAN *stands looking down at* COLUMBA *who fingers the bottom of his habit.*

GRILLAAN This has got to stop, Columba.
COLUMBA I had one foot in the boat and the other on dry land. When I jumped, the boat shot out from under me and down I went into the water. You should have heard Brendan laugh.
GRILLAAN I said this can't go on.
COLUMBA Luckily it was shallow water and I landed on my hands and knees.
GRILLAAN The Bishop of Perth was here again today to see you — that's twice in one week — and I had to tell him you were still out on visitation.

> COLUMBA *does not speak.*

Somebody every day. And I have to invent excuses for you: you are gone to Tiree; you are visiting Colonsay; you're away to Arran.
COLUMBA We have searched Tiree and Colonsay and Arran.
GRILLAAN At this very moment there are two men waiting to see you.
COLUMBA (*Listlessly*) Who are they?
GRILLAAN I don't know who they are. Look, Columba, there are at least a dozen things to be discussed and we never even get mentioning them.
COLUMBA What's wrong, Grillaan?
GRILLAAN Two of the novices are ill, very ill, and Sillan says he has tried all the cures he knows of.

COLUMBA I must call on them.

GRILLAAN The roof of the refectory could fall any minute. We need to repair the choir seats. Another message from Gregory of Bracholy: their crops all failed and they have only enough food to last them until the middle of next week. Cormac says he needs new sails for the big boat. And Dochonna — he's a danger to himself in that kitchen; some of these days he'll set fire to himself. What are we going to do about him? And the farm — there's no one competent to look after it since you took Brendan off on this wild goose chase of yours.

COLUMBA I'll find him yet, Grillaan.

GRILLAAN And Brendan — that's another thing.

COLUMBA What's wrong with Brendan?

GRILLAAN Have you looked at him recently? Have you looked at anything for the past two weeks?

COLUMBA What's wrong with Brendan?

GRILLAAN He's not eating. He's not sleeping. He's failed away to sticks. He's not half the man he was.

COLUMBA I thought he enjoyed being out in the boat.

GRILLAAN If he's with you — anywhere — he's happy. He was always like you, but now he models himself completely on you. Last night, Columba — you were in the chapel at the time — the young Swiss student said something to Brendan that annoyed him. I don't know what it was. But Brendan flew into a wild temper and only that I was there, he would have struck the Swiss boy. He could have been you — in the old days.

COLUMBA I'm trying, Grillaan, as God's my judge. I'm trying.

GRILLAAN (*Softly*) Give it up, Columba. Give it up. This obsession — it's bad for your body, it's bad for your soul. Oswald's gone. What matter? Not a month passes but a new student arrives. Forget him. We need you here, Columba. The monastery needs you. We all need you.

COLUMBA You gave me your advice, Grillaan, and I am trying to follow that advice. I keep the Rule like the most ardent youth on the island —

GRILLAAN How blind can you be. He came here because of you
— because of your reputation —

COLUMBA None of us knows that.

GRILLAAN And out there in the study hall at the moment are
forty young students who need you, who have heard
of the life you have founded and have left all to follow
it. You have a duty to them — ordinary sensible boys
who need you.

COLUMBA Give me one more day — that's all I ask — one more
day to search the Isle of Rhum.

GRILLAAN It's always one more with you — one more visit to
Derry, one more night in the chapel, one more appeal
from the family, one more territory to open up. Can
you never say no?

COLUMBA I could have started again with him. And instead of
that I was a scandal-giver.

GRILLAAN Tomorrow then and that's the end of it. (*Not unkindly*)
You're shivering with cold. Go to the kitchen and dry
yourself.

COLUMBA I'll see the two men who are sick first. Where are
they?

GRILLAAN You'll dry yourself first. Then I'll tell you where they
are.

COLUMBA *rises and goes towards the door.*

COLUMBA Iona would be lost without you, Grillaan.

GRILLAAN No, it wouldn't. I'm busy over many things. Go on
and dry yourself. We have enough patients in the
place as it is.

COLUMBA *goes off.* GRILLAAN *goes to the door to look
at him. Then returns. Sees the cloak on the bed. Lifts it.
It is wet, too. He is about to go off with it when*
EOGHAN *and* AEDH *enter.* EOGHAN *is Columba's
brother. They do not resemble each other in any way.*
EOGHAN *is small, lean and carries himself carelessly.
He has all the worst characteristics of a country man:
cunning, wary, watchful, smiling too easily. Yet he has
a gauche dignity, a quiet power that marks him out as*

61

a leader. He is dressed in rough brown tweeds. AEDH, *his son, a young man in his late twenties, is a finer figure. He is lightly built, holds himself well — almost arrogantly — and is obviously in a bad temper and anxious to be off. He has not much time for monks or monasteries.*

EOGHAN   It's only us again. Did he come back since?

GRILLAAN *treats them with courtesy — and no more.*

GRILLAAN   Yes. He's here now. Come in and take a seat. I'll get him for you.

EOGHAN   We had a stroll round there. Great place you have here. Powerful altogether.

GRILLAAN   A lot of improvements are needed. Most of the buildings haven't been touched since the day we put them up. Here's a stool here.

EOGHAN   It's a bed we need after that big meal you gave us.

GRILLAAN   He shouldn't be long. Your names are — ?

EOGHAN   This is Aedh, my son. And I'm his brother. Just tell him Ownie's here.

GRILLAAN   Eoghan and Aedh.

GRILLAAN *stops at the door.*

You've just come to see Columba and the island?

EOGHAN   That's it. I missed him when he was home last month.

GRILLAAN   There's nothing the matter at home, is there?

AEDH   Are you going to get him or are you not? We can't hang around this God-forsaken place all day!

EOGHAN   That'll do you, boy!

GRILLAAN   I'm not asking out of curiosity. And I would like to remind you that he is Columba of Iona and not Columba of Kilmacrenan.

GRILLAAN *goes off.*

AEDH   Who the hell does he think he is?

EOGHAN   Quiet. Quiet. Quiet.

AEDH Bloody cheek! Columba of Iona! You would think he was the Emperor of Rome or something!

>   AEDH *stands sullenly at the corner of the stage. His father moves about examining the room with all the curiosity and vague awe of a layman in a monastery. Occasionally, when he thinks he hears someone coming, he stands innocently looking at the table.* AEDH *takes no interest in what his father does.*

EOGHAN Draughty old place, isn't it? (*He feels the bed*) Stone, by God! If you slept on one of those things you wouldn't be so hard to get up in the morning. (*Moves over to the table. Looks up at the scrolls*) All them books! Powerful altogether. Powerful. (*Takes one down. Tries to read it. Cannot. Puts it back, looks at the crucifix. Taps it*) Just thought it was oak.

AEDH We're wasting our time here.

>   EOGHAN *examines a stool.*

EOGHAN Whoever made that was no craftsman.

AEDH I said we're wasting our time here.

EOGHAN I used to think when your mother died, may she rest happy, I used to think it would be a good idea to retire to a place like this.

AEDH Why didn't you?

EOGHAN And live on that stuff they gave us there now? What was it? Seal? No wonder Columba likes to come home now and again for his food. Still and all — no women, that's a big advantage.

AEDH That's good coming from you! Does your reverend brother know about the Fermanagh tramp you have living with you?

EOGHAN (*Nastily*) We're here because of your slut, Aedh, and don't forget it!

AEDH Because she wouldn't live under the same roof as a whore.

EOGHAN She'll be gone when we get back. I told her to clear out.

AEDH Then it will be another one — won't it?

EOGHAN Shut up! Here he is! And let me do all the talking!

AEDH Talk to your heart's content.

> COLUMBA *enters, followed by* GRILLAAN. *At the sight of his brother and nephew,* COLUMBA *brightens considerably. He is almost the old Columba again.* EOGHAN *wears his most pleasant smile.* GRILLAAN *stands watchfully at the side.*

EOGHAN Columba!

COLUMBA Eoghan! You're welcome! And Aedh! The pair of you —I'm delighted to see you! Have you been here long?

EOGHAN Only a wee while.

COLUMBA Your first visit to the island and I would have to be away! Have you eaten?

EOGHAN Up to here. (*Indicating his neck*) Man, but you're looking well!

COLUMBA Why wouldn't I with nothing to do and two hundred men to look after me?

EOGHAN Powerful. Powerful.

COLUMBA And Aedh! You're welcome to Iona, Aedh. They say at home he's like me, Grillaan, do you think so?

GRILLAAN Perhaps in temperament, Abbot.

COLUMBA God forbid, Aedh. With your father's looks and my temperament you would be in a poor way. Sit down. Sit down. What sort of a crossing had you? Did you come alone?

> COLUMBA *recovers his old form more strongly as time passes.*

EOGHAN We had no notion of coming here at all. The two of us were out after the pollock and when we found ourselves up round Malin Head, we thought we might as well nip over to see you when we were that near.

COLUMBA Not that old tub with the warped beam!

EOGHAN A good man can handle her.

COLUMBA You should go down to the slip and see this thing, Grillaan. You wouldn't put a waterhen out in her.

EOGHAN   She took us this length and she'll take us back.

COLUMBA   And did you pull the whole way?

EOGHAN   I'll grant you my arms are a wee bit tired.

COLUMBA   Strong as horses, these Tirconaill men! But tell me,
          Aedh — how's the baby — (*He tries to remember the
          name*) Donnchadh, that's it. (*To* GRILLAAN) You didn't
          know I was a grand-uncle, did you?

EOGHAN   Spoiled. Ruined. All it says is No, No.

COLUMBA   Well, we know who's fault that is. (*To* GRILLAAN) The
          last time I was there, he wouldn't let it down off his
          knee for a minute. (*To* AEDH) Is it going to be a
          Tirconaill man or an Antrim man?

EOGHAN   It's the spitting image of our father, God be good to
          him.

COLUMBA   (*Very pleased*) How could it be? A great-grandfather?

EOGHAN   I'm telling you — its eyes and its laugh and the way
          it holds its head to the side.

COLUMBA   Donnchadh will be a good man then — which
          reminds me —

          *He goes to the head of his bed and pulls out a box from
          which he takes a ring.*

EOGHAN   What is he at now?

COLUMBA   Something I've always intended doing since Donn-
          chadh was born. I forget to bring it with me each time
          I go over.

EOGHAN   (*To* AEDH) Thank him for the wee silver cross he sent
          the child.

AEDH   Thank you for the wee silver cross you sent the child.

COLUMBA   Don't mention it, Aedh. No, this is something
          different — something the heir to the family should
          have —

EOGHAN   What is it, Columba?

COLUMBA   It is a ring that was given by Patrick to Conall Culban,
          son of Niall Naoighiallach. And Conall Culban
          passed it down to his son, Fergus Ceannfada. And he
          to his son, Fedhlimidh, my father. And he to me. And
          now I to you, Aedh, for your son, Donnchadh, who
          will one day come to power, and rule strongly and

justly and wisely, with God's help.

> AEDH *takes the ring. He is embarrassed — by the gift and because of his moody silence up to this.*

AEDH Columba — thank you —

EOGHAN I often wondered where that ring went to.

> GRILLAAN *is assured that this is just a happy family reunion. He goes to door.*

GRILLAAN If there is anything you need, I'll be in the community room.

COLUMBA These men will be staying the night. Grillaan, will you look after them?

EOGHAN No, no, Columba, we can't stay the night. They would think at home we were drowned if we didn't turn up before dawn.

COLUMBA Who's to miss you? Ita's looking after the baby and you know very well she's glad to be rid of her cranky old father-in-law for a day or two.

EOGHAN We'll see then; we'll see.

> COLUMBA *waves to* GRILLAAN *to go. The matter is settled.* AEDH *stands examining the ring.*

COLUMBA That's settled then. It's seldom enough I see either of you. And talking of Ita, how is she, Aedh?

AEDH She's —

EOGHAN Fine, Columb — just fine —

COLUMBA She made a good convert, Ita. She's a credit to both of you and to your good Christian home.

> AEDH *looks at his father — defying him to speak.*

EOGHAN And you should see how she has taught the wee lad to bless himself.

COLUMBA Already?

EOGHAN And say the Our Father — after his own style, of course — grunting and blathering away yonder.

COLUMBA Her own people — they never forgave her, did they?

EOGHAN A thick crowd, them Antrim Picts. But they'll get over it. It will pass. (*Changing subject*) Man, this is a great place you've got here. Powerful altogether.

COLUMBA Had you a look around?

EOGHAN It would take you a week to see it right.

COLUMBA I'll show you over it in the morning. You're very quiet, Aedh. Have you the harvest in yet?

AEDH Most of it —

EOGHAN I see your own hay's all up.

COLUMBA For a change. We're always late here. Poor soil.

EOGHAN Where were you when we came?

COLUMBA I was out looking for one of the novices who — got lost.

EOGHAN On an island this size?

COLUMBA He was new here — about to begin. It's a beautiful ring, isn't it, Aedh?

AEDH *is tired of his father's hedging.*

AEDH Tell him the truth. Stop beating about the bush!

EOGHAN Aye — the truth — the truth —

COLUMBA What's this?

EOGHAN Well you see, Columb, it's like this here, you see, like this —

AEDH Ita's gone back to Antrim and taken the baby with her!

EOGHAN Let me tell it, let me tell it.

COLUMBA When did this happen?

EOGHAN Four or five days ago — nothing to worry about —

AEDH It was his idea that we come to you. I wanted to settle it my own way.

EOGHAN That's what I'm trying to avoid, Columb. His temper's as quick as your own. So what I says to him, I says, we'll do nothing hasty, I says. We'll go across to your uncle and he'll advise us what to do. You see yourself it's a tricky business like, her being a convert and now herself and the wee lad being held by them heathen Picts.

COLUMBA Held?

AEDH   Give me half a dozen men and I'll get her back.

EOGHAN   Do you see what I'm up against — rearing to fight the
          whole of Antrim single-handed.

COLUMBA   Tell me what happened.

EOGHAN   It all began with a bit of a row between the boy here
          and Ita — nothing much — just a bit of a tiff — you
          know what young couples are —   So up she gets
          this night, takes a horse and trap, and off with
          herself and the baby back home.

COLUMBA   She is a good wife and a good mother, Aedh?

AEDH   There isn't better.

COLUMBA   And you treated her properly?

AEDH   It was his fault, the whole thing, if he were man
          enough to admit it, and this was his idea — dragging
          you into it.

COLUMBA   Have you gone to bring her back?

AEDH   I went the length of the River Bann and a brother of
          hers met me there. They're not letting her back —
          neither her nor the child.

EOGHAN   So he came home to gather the clan and take her back
          by force and as soon as I heard that, I said we would
          come and see you.

COLUMBA   What can I do?

EOGHAN   Well you know yourself the feeling there is at home
          when he had to go and marry a Pict in the first place.

AEDH   She's better than many a Christian I could name!

EOGHAN   And that feeling hasn't died down yet. Many of them
          are saying no son of a Pict will lead them.

COLUMBA   If they respect Aedh, they'll respect Aedh's son.

AEDH   If they ever see him again.

COLUMBA   You'll have to go back and try again.

AEDH   I vowed I would — with an army.

EOGHAN   Big talk. You know you wouldn't get a handful to
          follow you.

COLUMBA   No, no, no, no. That's no solution. You'll have to go
          back alone, Aedh, and talk to them.

AEDH   I don't even know where they're holding her — could
          be anywhere in the Antrim mountains.

COLUMBA   It will be near Larne. Wasn't that her home place?

AEDH   What do you want me to do? Search the whole of the northeast coast myself?

EOGHAN No. He'll never get her back that way. They have her now and they'll keep her.

COLUMBA There's no other way.

EOGHAN You could get her back, Columb.

COLUMBA Me? How? Wait a minute — yes. Comgall of Bangor — his men work right up through that area —

EOGHAN That's not what I had in mind — what I was thinking was that you could — you know there — you could get the men together round Aedh and maybe you yourself would lead them over to —

COLUMBA You said you came for my advice, Eoghan.

AEDH Come on. He's not interested.

COLUMBA I am interested! You are my nephew and Donnchadh is my grand-nephew and the heir to Kilmacrenan. He must be got back. There is no question about that. But as to the best course —

EOGHAN (*Quickly*) Forty men would do it — half that with you at their head.

COLUMBA That day is over for me — finished.

EOGHAN I sounded them myself and they said they'll go but only if Columba is leading them.

COLUMBA No — no — finished — finished.

EOGHAN There'll be no fighting. All we need is a show of strength. Give me twenty good men with you in front and I'll show you the backside of a full army of Picts.

COLUMBA It is no way — no way —

EOGHAN Nothing to do but walk in and take the woman and the baby home to Tirconaill. Not a blow struck. Two days going and two days coming back. You'll be home in Iona by Sunday night.

COLUMBA No — no — no —

EOGHAN I know you don't want to fight or to have anything to do with fighting, Columb; neither does Aedh nor myself, and there will be no fighting — I promise you that. All we need to do to get the heir back is to show our courage, to prove that we're not afraid of a breed of savages, to show that we're sons of Kings and men of valour.

COLUMBA Valour has many meanings.

EOGHAN   And it is in God's cause that you are going to lead us
         — to save Ita and the baby from the heathens.

COLUMBA I'll go to Comgall — myself — tonight —

EOGHAN   My blood and yours and the blood of Fedhlimidh,
         our father, flows in the veins of that child, Columb.
         What would he say if he were standing here now —
         leave it to the Picts? Let it grow up a heathen, a
         stranger to the soft lands of Gartan? Let them keep it?
         Is that what he would say?

AEDH   I'm going home. I knew he didn't care.

COLUMBA I do care! I do care!

EOGHAN   Hugh is waiting for us at home and Seán Bán and
         young Turlough and the seven sons of Brian Ceann
         Dubh and the Cumines —

COLUMBA (*Surprised*) The two Cumines?

EOGHAN   This is family, Columb! Our family — his, yours,
         mine. And in a matter like this — a religious matter
         — all personal differences are forgotten. Yes, the
         Cumines that you routed a month ago, they are going
         to supply the horses and the food — provided you
         lead us.

COLUMBA Eoghan — Eoghan —

EOGHAN   Is it a bad thing we are asking of you — that you save
         two souls for the Church of God, that you unite under
         the banner of Christ the cousins that have fought
         against one another for generations? Is that a bad
         thing? That you do your priestly work of peace and
         salvation for your own family? Is that a bad thing?

COLUMBA I don't know — I don't —

EOGHAN   A young shepherd — a boy from Tory Island — lives
         on the slopes of Slemish mountain. We have been in
         touch with him. Three days from now he is to meet us
         at Coleraine to bring what news he can find out. He
         is a sharp lad and he will know exactly where they are
         being held. All we will have to do is bring them home
         in triumph.

         COLUMBA's *questions are half-voluntary, half-
         automatic.*

70

COLUMBA   They will be strongly guarded. The Picts are cunning warriors.

EOGHAN   They will expect us from the north. We can surprise them from the south.

COLUMBA   With twenty men?

EOGHAN   We'll rally a legion if you are leader.

COLUMBA   This Tory boy — can you trust him?

EOGHAN   He was baptized in your own church in Tory.

COLUMBA   His father's name?

EOGHAN   Canice, son of Colman.

COLUMBA   I knew him.

EOGHAN   We meet on Friday. If he says they are waiting for us, you will lead us south to Antrim town and from there up to the foot of the mountains.

COLUMBA   And the Cumines — they have forgotten their defeat?

EOGHAN   Family, Columb, family!

COLUMBA   We need fifty horses and enough food for three days.

EOGHAN   If we go south, it will take a week at least —

COLUMBA   In Tyrone we'll eat off the land. We need food only for the time in Antrim.

AEDH   He will wear the ring and be worthy of it, Columba!

EOGHAN   Like his grandfather and *his* grandfather and *his* grandfather!

> DOCHONNA *enters. He is doting. His habit is untidy. His expression strange, vacant.* COLUMBA *goes to him.*

DOCHONNA   It's Caornan, Columba — he's not about anywhere — I've gone right round the island and I can't find him —

COLUMBA   I want you to meet —

DOCHONNA   He's an old man, you see, and his sight's not so good and I'm afraid something might happen to him.

COLUMBA   He's in bed resting.

DOCHONNA   What's that?

COLUMBA   Caornan — he's asleep.

DOCHONNA   Asleep?

COLUMBA   In his room having a rest.

DOCHONNA   He's not as young as us, Columba. He tires easily.

COLUMBA   You are the youngest of the three of us.

DOCHONNA Aye, aye, aye, funny thing that — I'm the youngest. Do you know what we're going to do tomorrow, Caornan and me? It was his suggestion — he came in there to me in the kitchen and whispered it to me.

COLUMBA What are you going to do, Dochonna?

DOCHONNA Build a room for you. The Abbot should have a room of his own, a big room, the size of Finnian's.

COLUMBA But I have a room, Dochonna.

DOCHONNA That's what he whispered to me. The pair of us — I'll carry the stones and he'll do the building — for I've got the strength and he's got the head —

COLUMBA Yes, Dochonna, yes, yes —

DOCHONNA He says we'll make a great room for the Abbot where he can work and pray with no one to interfere with him — that's what he says.

> DOCHONNA *fades out and looks around bewilderedly.* COLUMBA *catches him by the arm and steers him towards the door.*

COLUMBA You are tired too, Dochonna. You have worked too hard.

DOCHONNA He can work and pray with no one to interfere with him — that's what Caornan says —

> DOCHONNA *goes off.* COLUMBA *watches him go.*

EOGHAN They're not all like that, are they?

COLUMBA That is a holy priest.

> COLUMBA *comes back into the room.*

AEDH We'll cross tonight and be home by tomorrow morning.

EOGHAN Seán Bán wants until Monday. He has to go to Innishowen to gather the Disert Eigne men.

AEDH And meet in Derry.

EOGHAN At the ferry at noon.

AEDH (*To* COLUMBA) We'll have too many now that you're in front of us!

EOGHAN   It will be a sight, man, a sight!

AEDH   And Antrim is rich! The booty there'll be!

EOGHAN   He'll lead us on his white horse and the road will open before him!

COLUMBA   (*Softly*) I'm not going.

EOGHAN   What?

AEDH   What did he say?

COLUMBA   I can't go! I can't go!

EOGHAN   Columba, son of Fedhlimidh —

COLUMBA's *speech is a plea — a pathetic appeal. He cannot refuse his family. He begs them to release him.*

COLUMBA   Look at me, brother, look at me. I am an old man. My arms are scarred by the wounds of battle. Look at them. And here — here is a heart that leaps when you call, and pounds against my ribs to join you and lead you and fight with you. But I have a soul, too, that whispers to me. I am small and puny, it says, because you have neglected me. And in a short time I will be standing before the King, it says, and I am pale and untried, it says. I am not reddened by blood, it says. Give me at least your failing years, it says, to battle with the flesh —

AEDH   You said you would go! You said it yourself!

COLUMBA   Leave me — please leave me —

AEDH   If you are a priest you'll go!

EOGHAN *signals to his son to keep quiet. He is still confident.*

EOGHAN   Columb, Columb, there are men there waiting for you, men who are straining for bloodshed. If you come with us you can prevent that bloodshed. But if you don't come, no man can hold them, no man. And there will be killing and torture and death; and men who have not confessed their sins for a twelvemonth will die in their guilt and be damned forever!

COLUMBA   For God's sake, leave me —

AEDH   Are you afraid? Is Columba a coward?

COLUMBA I am afraid to meet my God.

AEDH I told you he was no good! They're all old women in this place!

EOGHAN Columb —

COLUMBA I can't go, Eoghan — I can't go — I can't go —

EOGHAN I have fought with you in every battle you have ever fought.

COLUMBA Please —

EOGHAN At Culdrevny, at Coleraine, at Culfada last month.

COLUMBA *shakes his head: No. No. No.*

I never asked the why or wherefore but when the call came from my brother Columb, I answered it like a man and ran my risk with the rest.

COLUMBA I'll go to Comgall — yes, I'll speak to Comgall — today —

AEDH Come home, father! Can't you see he's a drivelling old woman!

EOGHAN'S *façade of pleasantness is dropped.*

EOGHAN You deny us, Columb? And your father's great-grandchild?

COLUMBA If Comgall can do anything —

EOGHAN And Gartan, your birthplace, and Kilmacrenan and Churchill, all Tirconaill — you deny it all?

COLUMBA I can't — I can't —

EOGHAN You deny them? You spit on them?

COLUMBA I have a soul —

EOGHAN Then we deny you, monk!

AEDH Leave him to his dotage!

EOGHAN And we curse you! And Kilmacrenan curses you! And Derry curses you! And Gartan that bred you curses you! And Innishowen curses you! And the whole of Tirconaill and Tyrone curse you for a traitor and a coward!

AEDH Leave him! Leave him!

EOGHAN And your father, Fedhlimidh, and your mother, Eithne, from their graves, they curse you, monk, for denying their own!

> EOGHAN *is white with fury.* AEDH *tries to pull him off stage.*

AEDH He's no good! He's no good! He has no time for anyone but himself!

EOGHAN May all your faculties fail you, monk. And may you end your days without food or friend on a barren rock without shade or shelter!

> AEDH *has pushed his father to the door. There he stops; takes the ring from his pocket and flings it across the stage.*

AEDH There! Take your ring and keep it!

EOGHAN And when you die, may no grave ever cradle your ungrateful remains. May the hawks eat your flesh and the dogs gnaw at your white bones! And may your work wither and die with you! And may my grandchildren and my great-grandchildren curse you every day they draw breath!

> AEDH *gets him off.* EOGHAN's *voice comes to* COLUMBA *standing alone in the centre of the stage.*

Coward! Traitor! Traitor! Traitor! Traitor! Traitor!

COLUMBA Get out of my monastery! Get out of my island! Get out of my life! Go back to those damned mountains and seductive hills that have robbed me of my Christ! You soaked my sweat! You sucked my blood! You stole my manhood, my best years! What more do you demand of me, damned Ireland? My soul? My immortal soul? Damned, damned, damned Ireland! — (*His voice breaks*) Soft, green Ireland — beautiful, green Ireland — my lovely green Ireland. O my Ireland —

> *He staggers back, drops on to a stool and lies across the table. Long pause. Silence.* BRENDAN *comes running in.*

BRENDAN Columba! Abbot, are you all right? I'll tear him asunder if he laid a hand on you. Are you hurt? Who let him in here? Who was he? Where was he from?

COLUMBA He was my brother — he was my brother from Kilmacrenan.

BRENDAN Did he strike you? Did he touch you?

COLUMBA He came to save me, Brendan. To make me a real exile.

BRENDAN If he ever puts his foot in this place again, I'll catch him by the back of his blue jacket and fling him into the tide!

COLUMBA He won't be back — ever again —

GRILLAAN *enters.*

GRILLAAN They're gone?

BRENDAN Lucky for them! Just let them come back here again!

GRILLAAN They made a lot of noise. (*To* COLUMBA) You wouldn't go?

COLUMBA You knew?

GRILLAAN I had a good suspicion.

COLUMBA They cursed me, Grillaan. They cursed and disowned me.

GRILLAAN I gathered the novices into the chapel to pray for you.

COLUMBA Bring me there, too, because I am empty.

COLUMBA *rises.* DOCHONNA *appears in the doorway.*

DOCHONNA Caornan! Caornan! I found him! I found him! In the cave on the east side!

GRILLAAN My God, what is he up to!

DOCHONNA Come in, Caornan! Come in!

OSWALD *enters, head down, emaciated, weary, ashamed of himself.*

Look at him, Columba, like something the sea washed up!

BRENDAN Oswald!

OSWALD I came back because I was hungry.

COLUMBA *breaks away from* GRILLAAN *and* BRENDAN *and runs to embrace the boy.*

COLUMBA Welcome — welcome home — welcome home, Oswald.

OSWALD There was nothing to eat but barnacles and dulse —

COLUMBA Oh, Oswald! Oswald! Oswald! Oswald!

DOCHONNA You said he was asleep, Columba, but I knew he wasn't. I knew he wasn't!

COLUMBA We were both asleep, Dochonna of Lough Conn! But we are awake now and ready to begin again — to begin again — to begin again!

Quick curtain.